# BOOK CLUB IN A BOX

M000084098

## Bookclub-in-a-Box presents the discussion companion for Audrey Niffenegger's novel
## The Time Traveler's Wife

Published in Canada by Vintage Canada, 2004, a division of Random House of Canada Limited. ISBN: 0-676-97633-6

Quotations used in this guide have been taken from the text of the paperback edition of **The Time Traveler's Wife**. All information taken from other sources is acknowledged.

This discussion companion for **The Time Traveler's Wife** has been prepared and written by Marilyn Herbert, originator of Bookclub-in-a-Box. Marilyn Herbert. B.Ed., is a teacher, librarian, speaker and writer. Bookclub-in-a-Box is a unique guide to current fiction and classic literature intended for book club discussions, educational study seminars, and personal pleasure. For more information about the Bookclub-in-a-Box team, visit our website.

### Bookclub-in-a-Box discussion companion for
### The Time Traveler's Wife
#### ISBN 10: 1-897082-26-6
#### ISBN 13: 9781897082263

This guide reflects the perspective of the Bookclub-in-a-Box team and is the sole property of Bookclub-in-a-Box.

CONTACT INFORMATION: SEE BACK COVER.

# BOOKCLUB-IN-A-BOX

## Audrey Niffenegger's The Time Traveler's Wife

# BOOKCLUB-IN-A-BOX

## Readers and Leaders Guide

Each Bookclub-in-a-Box guide is clearly and effectively organized to give you information and ideas for a lively discussion, as well as to present the major highlights of the novel. The format, with a Table of Contents, allows you to pick and choose the specific points you wish to talk about. It does not have to be used in any prescribed order. In fact, it is meant to support, not determine, your discussion.

## You Choose What to Use.

You may find that some information is repeated in more than one section and may be cross-referenced so as to provide insight on the same idea from different angles.

The guide is formatted to give you extra space to make your own notes.

# How to Begin

### Relax and look forward to enjoying your bookclub.

With Bookclub-in-a-Box as your behind the scenes support, there is little for you to do in the way of preparation.

Some readers like to review the guide after reading the novel; some before. Either way, the guide is all you will need as a companion for your discussion. You may find that the guide's interpretation, information, and background have sparked other ideas not included.

Having read the novel and armed with Bookclub-in-a-Box, you will be well prepared to lead or guide or listen to the discussion at hand.

Lastly, if you need some more 'hands-on' support, feel free to contact us. (See Contact Information)

# What to Look For

Each Bookclub-in-a-Box guide is divided into easy-to-use sections, which include points on characters, themes, writing style and structure, literary or historical background, author information, and other pertinent features unique to the novel being discussed. These may vary slightly from guide to guide.

INTERPRETATION OF EACH NOVEL REFLECTS THE PERSPECTIVE OF THE
BOOKCLUB-IN-A-BOX TEAM.

# Do We Need to Agree?
## THE ANSWER TO THIS QUESTION IS NO.

If we have sparked a discussion or a debate on certain points, then we are
happy. We invite you to share your group's alternative findings and experiences with us. You can respond on-line at our website or contact us through
our Contact Information. We would love to hear from you.

# Discussion Starters

There are as many ways to begin a bookclub discussion as there are mem-
bers in your group. If you are an experienced group, you will already have
your favorite ways to begin. If you are a newly formed group or a group
looking for new ideas, here are some suggestions.

Ask for people's impressions of the novel. (This will give you some idea
about which parts of the unit to focus on.)

- Identify a favorite or major character.

- Identify a favorite or major idea.

- Begin with a powerful or pertinent quote. (not necessarily from the
  novel)

- Discuss the historical information of the novel. (not applicable to all
  novels)

- If this author is familiar to the group, discuss the range of his/her
  work and where this novel stands in that range.

- Use the discussion topics and questions in the Bookclub-in-a-Box
  guide.

If you have further suggestions for discussion starters, be sure to share
them with us and we will share them with others.

# Above All, Enjoy Yourselves

# INTRODUCTION

Suggested Beginnings

Novel Quickline

Key to the Novel

Author Information

Punk,

Goth,

Rainer Maria Rilke

# INTRODUCTION

## Suggested Beginnings

**1.** The Time Traveler's Wife is often advertised as a science fiction story. **Into what category would you place this novel – science fiction? romance? fantasy? drama? Is there another category that it would fit into better?**

**2.** Niffenegger's book bends time, but not with the use of technology. Time is an arbitrary, man-made measure and the reader must choose whether or not to accept the belief that time in the novel does indeed bend and that Henry can travel back and forth. This idea is based on the difference between possibility and plausibility.
**When deciding whether or not to believe in Henry as a time traveler, consider the difference in the definitions of "possibility" and "plausibility".**

**3.** Niffenegger is primarily a product of the eighties, the period in which she grew up. She is a young and edgy artist and writer who believes that to portray life, her work should embody an element of strangeness and should include a slight change in the universe, as we know it.
**Who is her audience? Is this primarily a women's story, or can men also find something familiar in the characters and plot?**

**4.** Brad Pitt was the original choice as Henry in the movie of this novel. The character will now be played by Eric Bana.

**Do you agree with this casting? Who would you choose to play Clare, Ingrid, or Gomez?**

**5.** Many writers use themselves as models for their characters. The Time Traveler's Wife is not a biography in any way, but there are bits and pieces of Niffenegger in her characters.

**In which character(s) do you see Niffenegger?**

**6.** Claire is a cubist artist, which means that her portraits show the individual features of the person in a rearrangement of their separate pieces into an abstract form. Niffenegger does the same in the novel. She breaks time into its individual features and reorganizes them randomly.

**In what way can this technique contribute to the understanding of a relationship? Consider Niffenegger's combined artistic/literary style in your discussion of the novel's themes and characters.**

**7.** Despite the debate about which literary genre this novel fits into. Niffenegger claims she has written the ultimate love story.

**Do you agree or disagree?**

**8.** Henry feels strongly that one should not knowingly interfere with the future, yet this is just what he does with the lottery tickets.

**Consider this contradiction. is Henry's action wrong or immoral? If you could read the future, what would you do in Henry's situation?**

**9.** The most momentous event in Henry's life was his mother's death. Nothing could have prevented that, but Henry visits her from time to time.

**Is this time travel or memory or imagination? If you could know about the future, would you tell your present self everything? Would you make changes and what would they be?**

**10.** One of the novel's ideas is about "causality", the domino effect that leads from one event to another. The effect is that every decision we make has an impact.

**If Henry decided to stay in Ingrid's present, would she have lived? what effect would there have been if Henry had willingly told Clare all she wanted to know about the future?**

**11.** Clare spends much of her life waiting for Henry to return. Niffenegger says that true love, even when interrupted, will be rewarded some day.

**Is this a satisfactory outlook for our present times? Is there another reason why Clare only sees Henry in her very old age?**

**12.** Henry's time travel visits to his mother are fulfilling and painful at the same time. He loves to talk to her, even as a stranger. Perhaps it is a renewed opportunity for Henry to imagine what he would say to her now that he is grown.

**Consider the idea of such a renewed opportunity. would you use it, if it were offered? what might you say?**

# Novel Quickline

This is a love story of a married couple, Henry de Tamble, a punkish librarian, and Clare Abshire, an artist, who has a patient, serious demeanor. The story sounds ordinary so far, but like any unique love affair, this story is anything but ordinary. In Niffenegger's hands, theirs is a love story that strives to prove that love exceeds the physical boundaries of earth and body and that it exceeds the metaphysical boundaries of time.

Henry suffers from a rare genetic disorder that causes him to be suddenly and involuntarily transported to other scenes in his life, mostly in the past, and rarely into the future. This happens at times of stress or intense emotion. The first time Henry meets Clare, he's twenty-eight and she's twenty. The first time Clare meets Henry is when she is six and he's thirty-six. Separately their lives progress along their individual time-lines, but intersect one hundred and fifty-two times in a most unusual way: Henry always enters Clare's past; Clare enters Henry's present.

Niffenegger has put a whole different spin on the concept of love, relationships, and time. Her novel emphasizes the circular nature of time and the concept of our interconnected lives. Like Henry and Clare, the reader revisits certain scenes over and over again, but each time details unfold that keep the story fresh and developing. This is a story told with love and respect, an allegory to remind us that not all love, nor life, is explainable and nor, according to Niffenegger, should it be.

# Key to the novel       *... time and love as one*

In her novel, Niffenegger pairs time and love in a poetic structure that she presents to all lovers. Past and present are placed together in order to demonstrate our ongoing and universal hope for a better future. We are all captured by time and by love, two ideas that are normally considered separately; this novel captures the essence of both at the same time.

To do this, Niffenegger anchors her story with a large number of quotes and references by her favorite writers and poets and from archetypal stories. She opens the novel with two epigraphs by J.B. Priestley and Derek Walcott, respectively, then divides her story into three parts, using the thoughts of Rainer Maria Rilke and A.S. Byatt to introduce the successive sections.

The novel ends with thoughts from Homer's *Odyssey* .

- First epigraph from J. B. Priestley's, *Man and Time'*

  > *Clock time is our bank manager, tax collector,*
  > *police inspector; this inner time is our wife.*

- Second epigraph is from a poem by Derek Walcott, *Love After Love'*

  > *The time will come*
  > *When, with elation,*
  > *You will greet yourself arriving*
  > *at your own door, in your own mirror,*
  > *And each will smile at the other's welcome*
  >
  > *... Give back your heart*
  > *to itself, to the stranger who has loved you*
  > *all your life, whom you ignored*
  > *for another, who knows you by heart ...*
  > *Sit. Feast on your life.*

- Rilke's *Ninth Duino Elegy* (an excerpt in translation) opens **Part I,** *The Man Out of Time,* (p.6) of the novel.

  > *Oh, not because happiness exists, that too-hasty*
  > *profit snatched from approaching loss.*
  >
  > *But because truly being here is so much; because*
  > *everything here apparently needs us, this fleeting*
  > *world, which in some strange way keeps calling to*
  > *us. Us, the most fleeting of all.*
  >
  > *... Ah, but what can we take along into that other*
  > *realm? Not the art of looking, which is learned so*
  > *slowly, and nothing that happened here. Nothing.*
  > *The sufferings, then. And, above all, the heaviness,*
  > *and the long experience of love, -- just what is*
  > *wholly unsayable.*

- **Part II** is called *A Drop of Blood in a Bowl of Milk* (p.271) and again quotes Byatt.

A.S. Byatt, from her novel, **Possession**.

> *"What is it? My dear?"*
>
> *"Ah, how can we bear it?"*
>
> *"Bear what?"*
>
> *"This. For so short a time. How can we sleep this time away?"*
>
> *"We can be quiet together, and pretend–since it is only the beginning–that we have all the time in the world."*
>
> *"And every day we shall have less. And then none."*
>
> *"Would you rather, therefore, have had nothing at all?"*
>
> *"No. This is where I have always been coming to. Since my time began. And when I go away from here, this will be the mid-point, to which everything ran, before, and <u>from</u> which everything will run. But now, my love, we are here, we are <u>now</u>, and those other times are running elsewhere."*

- **Part III**, *A Treatise on Longing*, (p.497) opens with both Byatt and Rilke.

A.S. Byatt, from her novel, **Possession**.

> *His forty-third year. His small time's end. His time*
> *–*
> *Who saw Infinity through the countless cracks*
> *In the blank sin of things, and died of it.*

Rainer Maria Rilke, from *Going Blind* (an excerpt in translation).

> *She followed slowly, taking a long time,*
> *as though there were some obstacle in the way;*
> *and yet: as though, once it was overcome,*
> *she would be beyond all walking, and would fly.*

- These words from Homer's *The Odyssey* (excerpt in translation) close the love story of Henry and Clare.

> *Now from his breast into his eyes the ache*
> *of longing mounted, and he wept at last,*
> *his dear wife, clear and faithful, in his arms,*
> *longed for as the sun warmed earth is longed for by*
> *a swimmer*
> *spent in rough water where his ship went down*
> *under Poseidon's blows, gale winds and tons of sea.*
> *Few men can keep alive through a big surf*
> *to crawl, clotted with brine, on kindly beaches*
> *in joy, in joy, knowing the abyss behind:*
> *and so she too rejoiced, her gaze upon her husband,*
> *her white arms round him pressed as though*
> *forever.*

- Thus time and love are merged. When looked at closely, these quotes tell us to live for the moment because one never knows where the moments will go, and if one is lucky enough to find a heart's companion, make the most of it. Life, the ultimate romantic dream, is worth having on any terms, even for a short while. A comfortable love transcends time and is worth waiting for.

- This is exactly how she ends the novel, both for Clare and for herself.

> *I sit at the dining room table with a cup of tea, looking at the water, listening. Waiting.*

notes

*Today is not much different from all the other days ... it's not much different from the many other times he was gone, and I waited, except that this time I have instructions: this time I know Henry will come, eventually. I sometimes wonder if this readiness, this expectation, prevents the miracle from happening. But I have no choice. He is coming, and I am here.* (p.518)

- In her acknowledgements, Niffenegger ends with with the same thought in reference to her boyfriend, Christopher Schenberger: *I waited for you, and now you're here.*

# Author and Background Information

## Audrey Niffenegger

- *The Time Traveler's Wife* has received many good reviews and quite a bit of recognition. Niffenegger has been given a number of Arts Council grants, but her favorite is from a place called the Ragdale Foundation, an artist's retreat in the Lake Forest area, just thirty minutes from downtown Chicago. There is space for two hundred writers, visual artists and composers, who can stay, work, talk, and mingle, for the exorbitant rate of $25 per day. Niffenegger has received nine grants from this organization.

- Niffenegger was born in 1964 and grew up in Evanston, Illinois, just north of Chicago, where she was educated. She did a Bachelor of Fine Arts degree at the School of Art Institute of Chicago in 1985 and a master's level degree at Northwestern University, also in the Chicago area, in 1991.

- She is currently a visual artist and teacher, working at the Columbia College Chicago Center for Book and Paper Arts and teaching writing to the visual art students in the MFA program. This program focuses on merging text and images, for example, in full-length comics and visual novels such as **Maus** by Art Spiegelman. Her own artistic work, consisting of drawings, paintings, photos, and collages, is often on display at the Printworks Gallery in Chicago. She also has some pieces in the collection of the Newberry Library, the place where Henry works, including her own visual novel, **The Three Incestuous Sisters**. This book contains eighty hand-colored etchings, bound in calf skin by Niffenegger herself. Ten limited edition copies were made, but it has recently been mass produced and can now be enjoyed by a wider audience.

- Given where she was born, educated, lives, works and relaxes, Niffenegger's life boundaries are obviously quite small. Clearly it is her imagination that soars.

- Her many varied interests also include gardening and taxidermy. She owns several small-scale stuffed objects and she loves all things alternative – mummies, circus freaks, mutants, amputation, and she would call herself a bit of a punker. (see Punk Culture, p.17) She claims that none of the book is autobiographical except for the interests and the poems that she loves, which are echoed throughout the novel.

- Originally, Niffenegger thought to create Ingrid in her own image, but as the book progressed, she felt that Ingrid changed in too many ways. So she looked to the other characters. At times, she aligns herself closely in temperament with Henry, because it is Henry who shares her love for punk rock, which is the music of her times – the seventies and eighties. Niffenegger and Clare share a love of sculpture. Niffenegger is a fine artist (printmaking, paper, etchings), whereas Clare makes large-scale figures.

- When she finished writing the book, Niffenegger dyed her hair red. This was in homage to Clare and was a way of saying goodbye to both her and to the book.

- Niffenegger has a boyfriend, Christopher Schenberger, to whom she acknowledges thanks, but they do not live together. Instead she lives in her own place, with her two cats. Christopher's talents are diverse – he is an artist, musician, filmmaker and teacher, who also teaches at the Columbia College in Chicago. He is a drummer with a rock group called Avocet. She only met her boyfriend, Christopher, as she ended the writing of the book – a fitting conclusion!

- She is currently working on a new novel, **Her Fearful Symmetry** (working title), set in London, near Highgate cemetery. The book is about twin mirror-image girls, who inherit a flat on the edge of the cemetery. The setting of this novel is in keeping with what she refers to as her *natural Goth sensibility.*

- The movie rights for **The Time Traveler's Wife** were bought by Brad Pitt and Jennifer Aniston before the book was released. The film is currently in pre-production and should be released in 2008. The screen writer is Jeremy Leven who did such films as **Don Juan De Marco, The Notebook, Alex and Emma,** and **The Legend of Bagger Vance.** The film will be directed by Robert Schwentke of Germany and is scheduled to star Canadian actress, Rachel McAdams and Australian actor, Eric Bana.

# Punk Culture

- Punk culture evolved in the mid 1970s as a response to the popular music of the former hippie subculture of the 1960s and the heavy-metal music that developed soon after. There were many variations of style, but the message was essentially the same – it was subversive and often anarchistic. It dealt with social and political topics, such as the oppression of the lower classes. The fashion style associated with this music also varied and changed over time, but the original "classic" punk included, among many other elements, the following: combat or Doc Marten boots, tapered jeans or tight leather pants, ripped T-shirts, leather jackets, safety pins and body piercings, and longer hair. Some followers of punk later sported mohawk hairstyles and/or brightly colored hair. It was all intended as a rebellion against mainstream culture and the fashion of the day. Punk rockers initally drew their influence from groups such as The Doors, The Rolling Stones and The Velvet Underground, and then in the mid-1970s turned to groups like The Sex Pistols and The Ramones. What these groups have in common is the use of their sound as a statement of attitude. The sound matches their look and their message.

# Goth Culture

- From punk, music continued into Goth. Fans of Goth changed their fashion from the distressed look of the punkers with their ripped clothing and heavy footwear to the monochromatic black look of *The Sisters of Mercy, Marilyn Manson, and Batcave.* The fashion included heavy eye makeup, Renaissance-style clothing, and full-length leather trench coats. The jewellery changed from symbols of oppression (chains) to symbols of death (skullbones). The fashion also reflected a fascination with asexual or androgynous men and women.

- The modern-day Goth subculture first became popular in the early 1980s and continued into the '90s. Goth differs from punk in that it is more introspective in its concerns, which are seen as trying to come to terms with the "darker" aspects of human life – death and the questioning of what is "normal".

- The subculture is often perceived by mainstream society as representing an unhealthy fascination with death and the religious concepts of witchcraft (Wicca) and Satanism. However, this is seen by most Goths as a simplistic misrepresentation. Many Goths are Christian, and it is clear that like all cultures, subcultures, and religions, there are many variations and distortions.

- Goth music shows some influence from older literary movements, such as Romanticism, existential philosophy, and nihilism, as well as from the Gothic literature of the nineteenth century. Examples include the work of Mary Shelley *(Frankenstein)*, Bram Stoker *(Dracula),* and the poetry of Edgar Allan Poe, Shelley, and even Lord Byron.

- Music, like time, continues to ebb, flow, and change.

notes

## Rainer Maria Rilke

- Clare's favorite poet, Rilke, lived from 1875 to 1926 and is considered the greatest lyric poet of modern Germany. He created the **object poem**, which tries to describe a physical object so clearly that it removes the object from its locked position in time and space. As Rilke says, *"works of art ... are products ... of having gone to the very end in an experience, to where man can go no further."* It is also easy to see why Niffenegger, as both an artist and a writer, favors him.

# CHARACTERIZATION

Henry

Clare

Alba

Richard, Dr. Kendrick

Gomez, Charisse

Kimy

Ingrid

# CHARACTERIZATION

## Henry

- Henry de Tamble is a punkish librarian, who works at the Newberry Library in Chicago. When he is not shelving books he is falling in and out of the stacks, sometimes naked, but always to the consternation of his boss.

- He is the child of a very happily married couple, Richard (a violinist) and Annette (an opera singer). Annette dies in a car accident on Christmas Eve when Henry is five. This is the first time he travels in time and space – he finds himself unharmed, outside of the car that killed his mother. This event is so pivotal in Henry's life that he finds himself coming back to it over and over again. For Richard, time has become frozen. He becomes a figurative black hole, out of which there is nothing for Henry to grasp onto for support. Richard is waiting, not necessarily for Annette to return, but for release from his own nightmare of time.

- Henry first meets Clare in his present, when he is twenty-eight. But in his time travels, she meets him when she is six. He only travels into her past once he actually knows her, not before. In actual fact, he is only able to time travel into the lives of those who are important to him – Clare, his mother, Alba, Ingrid, and himself.

- Henry falls through time naked, suffering many bumps and bruises along the way. Niffenegger has not painted him as a superhero but as an ordinary man who uses his wits, intelligence, and physical skills to match the circumstances in which he finds himself. As time goes on and he gets older, his reflexes slow down. He's tired and worn, just like the rest of us, only in his case, his "disease" or condition accelerates his situation.

- Henry suffers from what Dr. Kendrick calls chrono-impairment. There is something wrong with Gene # 17. Henry's condition is triggered by stress, which is a very plausible factor. Henry and Alba are both CDP (Chronologically Displaced People) – they love another time and place. **(p.374)** Henry often finds himself *"dislocated in time, for no reason."* **(p.140)** He spends much of his time traveling back to events and to people who have been important to him. *"I tend to go to the past, rather than the future."* **(p.162)** This is also a feature indicative of dreams. **(see Dreams, p.52 )**

- Henry has his own *"Special Theory of Time Travel as Performed by Henry DeTamble"*. He considers his condition to be similar to epilepsy, primarily because there are physical cues that indicate its onset, such as stress. Flashing lights and speed can also affect him.

- There are a number of other ways of looking at Henry.

    o Henry is good at picking locks, which is a metaphor for picking the locks of time.

    o Clare's grandmother thinks he is a new kind of human– in her view, a demon. She foreshadows Clare's future role in her relationship with Henry by referring to the Odysseus/Penelope

connection. *"In fairy tales, it is always the children who have adventures, the mothers have to stay at home and wait."* (p.126)

o Henry's view of meeting Henry: *"He is me, but I'm not him yet."* (p.148) This could be anyone looking back on their childhood.

o Henry with Henry thinking of Clare: *"I am a close approximation that she guides towards a me that exists in her mind's eye. What would I be without her?"* (p.149)

- There are two mysteries about Henry: How does Clare become pregnant, and when will he die?

  o Henry has a vasectomy at age thirty-six, but he revisits Clare and sleeps with her when he's thirty-three. That is how he impregnates her successfully. (p.356)

  o Alba tells Henry that he will die when she is five.

# Clare

- We meet Clare as a child, when she meets Henry for the first time. Then we more or less follow her life chronologically up to and beyond the time that Clare, the adult, meets Henry. The reader is right beside Clare, anticipating the moment when they actually meet in the present. But Henry does not know her. (see Henry, 23)

  *I'm at a loss because I am in love with a man who is standing before me with no memories of me at all. Everything is in the future for him.* (p.8)

- Clare is sustained by a list of one hundred and fifty-two dates, beginning September 23, 1977 and ending May 24, 1999. The list was dictated to Clare by Henry, and comprises all of the dates when he will enter her life. But it ends two years before Henry actually meets

Clare in his present. She needs that time to live without Henry as an experiment, to see if there can be someone else in Henry's place and to see if this relationship will work.

- The story is an 'Alice-in-Wonderland' parallel, time-wise instead of size-wise. It also fits with the element of the Alice story that was, of course, that Alice's adventures were all a dream. The entire story could conceivably be Clare's dream. On the other hand, Clare is Penelope, waiting and creating art in the same way that Penelope wove and unwove her tapestries while waiting for Odysseus to return.

- Unlike Henry's family, Clare's family is intact but is not necessarily happy. We learn that her parents had a shotgun wedding, which corresponds to the situation of Clare's brother, Mark, and his fiancée. Her sister, Alicia, is the musician, a younger parallel to Annette.

- Clare's home is central to the story, because it is in the considerably large meadow on the property that Clare meets Henry. The meadow itself, surrounded by a woods, is a place of contradictions – it is simultaneously a place of peace and a place where peace is disturbed, first by Henry's visit, and then by Henry's death.

- Clare's whole existence is wrapped up in Henry. As she explains to Gomez, *"I love him. He's my life. I've been waiting for him, my whole life, and now, he's here."* (p.146) Her explanation is believable, but it could also be Clare's fantasy come true. Perhaps she had always imagined someone like Henry and then simply found him as an adult. *"...our lives are all tangled together, my whole childhood was different because of him."* (p.146) Because of the strength of her love, Clare anchors Henry in time and he travels less while he is with her.

- Clare becomes pregnant on the seventh try, lucky seven, the roll of the dice. Niffenegger points out that one should never give up on one's dreams, because it could all boil down to luck. The number seven has many symbolic meanings, including a Japanese reference to

notes

the seven gods who represent earthly happiness.

- Niffenegger tosses out the question of a parallel universe, or the place where we can consider what might happen if we do things differently. **If Henry's father had been a better father, more anchored in the present than in the past, would Henry have traveled less? At all?**

- The child is always more intense than the parent, and Alba's experiences are slightly more advanced than Henry's. She is working toward a future species of CDPs.

# Alba

- Alba's name was chosen because it means a *"white city. An impregnable fortress on a white hill."* (p.370) She symbolizes purity, innocence, and the strength that will enable her to face her future.

- At the time of her birth, Henry suffers from the extreme stress of joy and travels forward for the first time, *"an unusually high-quality slice of forward time travel."* (p.371) He sees Alba on a school trip when she tells him that her daddy is dead, but *"not continuously dead."* (p.373) Henry uses this information to reassure Clare and also himself. Although Alba gives Henry information about his future, Henry is comfortable with the thought that Alba and Clare will be all right. He knows now that he has to make the most of the little time remaining to him.

- Alba is part of Clare's and Henry's gift to each other. Just as Clare anchors Henry in his present, so Alba will anchor Clare in her future. She will have someone who will stay, *"stay and be there always ... so that when he was gone he wouldn't be entirely gone, there would be a bit of him with me ..."* (p.314) Henry feels exactly the same: *"... when I am snatched away from her, a part of me would remain."* (p.314)

- After Alba's birth, Clare does a pastel drawing of the infant. *"... the Alba in the drawing suddenly becomes three-dimensional, [and] leaps off the page."* (p.393) The picture is significant because for Clare it will remain as a record of her love for her daughter and through her daughter for Henry. *"It will say, we made you, and here you are, here and now."* (p.394) This drawing will lock Alba into time.

- Alba has the same syndrome as Henry and can also time travel, but she is a new generation with more control, more confidence, more strength of character. Her experiences are slightly more advanced, perhaps because she has much more support than Henry ever did. In addition to having Henry, Alba has Clare's understanding and acceptance of her condition plus the expertise of Dr. Kendrick. Alba also gets a list of dates from Henry but has the pleasure of sometimes time traveling with him.

- Sadly, when she loses Henry, she is also the same age as he was when Annette, his mother, died.

## Richard

- With the death of his beloved wife, Richard becomes locked in time. He can no longer function as a father and eventually ceases to function as a musician. He becomes an alcoholic through *"twenty-three years of determined drinking ..."* (p.217) Alcohol helps Richard obliterate time, as it does for Henry too until he meets Clare.

- The love between Richard and Annette is mirrored and juxtaposed in Henry and Clare. Where the first couple is controlled by time, the second couple takes time into their personal sphere of power as much as possible. We may not be able to dominate time, but time can be manipulated in various ways.

- Richard eventually thaws enough to give Henry his mother's wedding rings and to be a good grandfather to Alba. She has inherited her musical skills from her grandparents.

# Dr. Kendrick

- Dr. Kendrick is a geneticist and a philosopher, who tries to help first Henry then Alba. The philosophical side of him is essential, because it points out that even science must be approached and understood from an emotional perspective. He embodies the idea of belief before, or instead of, proof. He could have dismissed Henry's time traveling story because of lack of evidence, but when Henry foreshadows the birth of Dr. Kendrick's Down Syndrome son, he chooses to believe. Choosing to believe is essential to Niffenegger's story.

- Choice is part of the physical world but becomes a trickier subject in the metaphysical world. It is not choice or fate that causes Henry's time travels. *"Things get kind of circular, when you're me. Cause and effect get muddled."* (p.303) (see Time Travel (science), p.62)

- Dr, Kendrick confirms this by telling Henry about "clock genes" which *"govern circadian rhythms [that] keep you in sync with the sun, that sort of thing."* (p.310) When these clock genes are thrown off track so is the body's inherent sense of time. Dr. Kendrick is about to experiment with creating mice that defy the rules of time. This is the essence of science that has the aim of defying not only the rules of time, but the rules of life, in order to see beyond.

# Gomez and Charisse

- Gomez and Charisse are friends of Clare and then become friends of the couple, Clare and Henry, once they are together. Although Gomez is married to Charisse, he has always been in love with Clare. When he meets Henry through Clare, he realizes that he had already met Henry with Ingrid. What he didn't know was that this was before Henry actually meets Clare in his present. This bit of *déjà vu* is a little of Henry's *"future seeping into now."* (p.422) Gomez doesn't like this Henry and tries hard to persuade Clare out of her relationship with him.

- Gomez has multiple opinions about Henry, none of them very good. Nevertheless, he rescues Henry a few weeks after meeting him at Clare's place.

  *'I know a lot of people who know you. People; well, women. Women who know you. ... They say some pretty strange things.'*

  *"I want to know why a seemingly mild-mannered librarian beats a guy into a coma over nothing while wearing kindergarten-teacher clothing. I want to know why Ingrid Carmichel tried to kill herself eight days ago. I want to know why you look ten years older right now than you did the last time I saw you ... I want to know why you can pick a Yale lock. I want to know why Clare had a photograph of you before she actually met you."* (p.138, 139)

  Henry decides to confide in Gomez because he knows that he needs a friend who will rescue him from the certainty of future consequences, resulting from the uncertain events in which Henry will find himself.

- Gomez and Clare make desperate love for the last time when Henry is already gone. In the middle of the session, Clare calls Gomez "Henry". *"Everything stops. A clock is ticking loudly."* (p.507) Clare is distraught and asks, rightly, what she has allowed herself to become when she has sex with her friend's husband. *"An answer comes, of sorts: You are the traveler now."* (p.508) There are all kinds of travelers.

# Kimy

- Mrs. Kim is Henry's neighbor and substitute parent. She has taken good care of both Henry and Richard since the accident. Until Henry travels back to see her during the time that he and Clare are trying to get pregnant, Henry never wondered about her personal situation. Mrs. Kim had a daughter who died of leukemia.

- Mrs. Kim is present in the novel to remind readers that family relationships can be made out of non-blood ties too. Sometimes in our lives we do not get to choose who we can travel with; sometimes the travelers choose us.

# Ingrid

- Ingrid is Henry's former girlfriend. They enjoy each other's company during certain shared activities, like music and dancing, but neither is the other's soul mate. Their individual needs are too divergent, and they can not cross the gulf of time and space between them.

- Both are in physical and emotional pain *"By entirely separate processes we have arrived at the same condition."* (p.474) When Henry revisits Ingrid's last day, he is powerless to stop her death. He had always maintained that people could not and should not interfere with the future. If Ingrid had lived, then all their lives would have been altered.

- Henry returns to tell Clare that Ingrid is dead. She reminds him that *"Ingrid's been dead for a long time ...'* [Henry responds,] *"Years, minutes ... same thing."* (p.478) Perhaps Henry has been dreaming. (see Dreams, p.52)

# FOCUS POINTS AND THEMES

## State of Being

## Free Will

## Marriage

# FOCUS POINTS AND THEMES

Independence is a large and defining feature of Niffenegger's personality and her present way of life, so it is not unusual to find her exploring that theme in both her art work and in her writing. **The Time Traveler's Wife** looks at the individual's state of being, marriage, and free will, in juxtaposition to the concept of independence. Her conclusions are revealing and, at the same time, surprisingly different.

## State of Being

- Clare and Henry, the novel's main characters, move around in life and space quite differently from each other. Clare's life unfolds in a normal, chronological way, while Henry's jumps around in time and place. His fragmented state of being is a direct contrast to Clare's continuous one. Niffenegger looks at how their differences work in their relationship.

- Henry is always moving around, while Clare is not. He won't travel on a plane because it moves too fast and it might throw him out of his present state of being. On the other hand, Henry also explains to Clare that when something has more mass it becomes gravitational and resists movement. Smaller things can go into orbit faster, which is why Henry did not die in the car accident, he was thrown clear. This is key for Henry in another sense – his mother's death was a pivotal event in his life, and he keeps orbiting around it trying to see it from every angle imaginable so as to understand it better. He is exploring his state of being.

- Clare is the sun around which Henry's moon revolves. He is the satellite to her stationary planet. But this state of fluctuation initially bothers both of them. Clare, especially, is frustrated by not knowing what will happen next.

  > *Why has he gone where I cannot follow?* (Clare, prologue)

  > *I hate to be where she is not, when she is not. And yet,*
  > *I am always going, and she cannot follow.* (Henry, prologue)

  The "state of being" can include life, time travel, or it can even mean death.

- Niffenegger is careful to explain that Henry's ability to time travel does not mean he can foresee, influence, or change the future, (although there is the question of his lottery winnings and giving Gomez stock tips ....). As Henry tells Gomez, *"Things happen once, only once ... if you are in time, not knowing [the future] ... you're free. Trust me."* (p.142) Niffenegger is using time travel as a sensory image, so that her characters try to experience each moment in time more fully and more intensely. Niffenegger concludes that when viewed in this way, a person's individual state of being can make a relationship more intense and interesting.

- After Clare meets Richard for the first time, she and Henry are so happy that the visit went well that they go to the playground and climb on the swings, sitting facing opposite directions.

*... we swing higher and higher, passing each other, sometimes in synch and sometimes streaming past each other so fast it seems like we're going to collide ... nothing can ever be sad, no one can be lost, or dead, or far away: right now we are here, and nothing can mar our perfection, or steal the joy of this perfect moment.* "(p.232)

Theirs is a state of being at its best.

# Free Will

- Having established the state of being, Niffenegger then moves to the concept of free will and asks how it fits into a philosophy that views everything in life as pre-ordained.

- Niffenegger does believe that we are all trapped by our past, by our memories, and by our genetic makeup. But she believes that free will can be exerted as an antidote to these things. As Henry tells Clare, we have free will only in the present. And, of course, life as we know it is only in the present.

- Henry refuses to tell Clare, or anyone, anything because knowing things ahead of time eliminates free will and can distort your life. *"Things happen. Knowing about them in advance makes everything...weird. You can't change anything, anyway."* (p.142) If Henry is right that the future cannot be changed, then perhaps we should have that knowledge. In that way, we might be able to change our reactions and be better able to cope. By not knowing, we are trapped in a time not of our making.

**What are your thoughts on this subject?**

notes

# Marriage

- The ideas of independence and marriage are not contradictory, although the common perception of marriage is based on the romantic notion of linked and interconnected lovers. Niffenegger presents her lovers as distinct entities moving in and out of a sphere that then crosses into a part of each of their individual spheres; that is, they connect on some levels, but not all. Clare cannot go with Henry, and Henry cannot always stay with Clare.

- This book is about what marriage means to the married partners who are not locked in step with each other. Henry is not only married to Clare, he is also married to time. This idea then reaches over toward Clare, who eventually becomes not only Henry's widow, but time's widow. Her future appears to be that she is to live according to someone else's clock.

- For Henry, Clare anchors him to the present. Without her, he might be flying off in many more directions. She holds him in the present. *"Being physically connected the way that we are, it's kind of rewiring my brain."* (p.225) And perhaps, in the end, that is what we all would like from our important relationships.

- As we know, Niffenegger herself is not married, nor has she ever been. She is only now in a new, wonderful relationship, after having dated a slew of oddball characters. When she began this book, she was in between relationships – lonely and waiting. She wanted desperately to think positively about lucky love, although she considers herself as having been unlucky in love. At precisely this point, her grandparent's relationship came into her mind. This novel is dedicated to her grandparents, Elizabeth and Norbert Tamandl. Norbert died young and was outlived by his wife for thirty years. She never remarried.

- Niffenegger wanted to write about a perfect marriage that is tested by something outside the control of the couple. The title came to her

notes

out of the blue, and from the title came the characters and then the story. She actually visualized the entire last scene before she wrote even one word.

- Despite the role model provided by her own grandparents, Niffenegger does not believe in the idea of "soul mates" in the traditionally romantic way, something in which Clare clearly does believe. Niffenegger tends to think of soul mates as being a merging of the parts of two souls, and she hopes that she successfully presents this idea in an edgier, more alternative way. Her quotes from Rilke and from A.S. Byatt's novel, **Possession**, explore this idea.

- The other source that she leans on heavily is Homer's story of Odysseus and Penelope. Odysseus (Ulysses) has left Penelope and his son, Telemachus, to go to war against Troy. He is away for ten years, and then, suddenly, the gods send him on another ten-year adventure before he is allowed to return home. Meanwhile, Penelope waits at home, weaving shrouds and keeping her potential suitors at bay. She promises to answer these suitors when her shroud is finished, but she weaves by day, and then unravels it by night, Eventually, the lovers are reunited – love is requited and satisfied.

- This idea of waiting is central to the novel and supports the idea of marriage as an integrated relationship of two souls. Just as Penelope waits for Odysseus, so Clare waits for Henry. However, Henry also waits for Clare to grow up and come into his present. Niffenegger, herself, was finished with waiting, but then her present boyfriend showed up three days after this novel's manuscript was completed.

- Waiting might be part of marriage but does not necessarily define it. Niffenegger concludes that love is worth waiting for, no matter what form it takes or what length of time it occupies. This novel is about the romantic notion of loyalty and patience, which are rewarded in the end. The form that such a reward takes is up for discussion.

**How do these ideas fit your own?**

notes

# WRITING STYLE AND STRUCTURE

## Literary Genre (sci fi)

## Style of Writing

## Structure

# WRITING STYLE AND STRUCTURE

## Literary Genre  *science fiction*

- One dictionary definition of science fiction describes the genre as *"dealing principally with the impact of actual or imagined science upon society or individuals, or more generally, literary fantasy including a scientific factor as an essential ... component."* (Merriam) Time travel is a real phenomenon under current investigation by the scientific community. (see Time Travel, p.62)  Although **The Time Traveler's Wife** is also considered to be romance, fantasy, and drama, the novel's premise turns on time travel.  According to this definition, the novel qualifies as science fiction.

notes

- There are other valid and historical reasons for calling this novel science fiction.

  o There are two historical perspectives on science fiction. Some critics trace the genre back to the classic and medieval works of imagination and speculation, and therefore place these works into science fiction fantasy. Others look at true science fiction as being based on a system of applied science and technology.

  o Both of these perspectives place the origins of science fiction firmly into the nineteenth century.

- The nineteenth century was the greatest period in history for technological advance. With it, writers and artists, who are the "canaries" of the world – the early warning system, began to worry about the potential for human and natural disaster. They felt that unlimited scientific advancement would produce irreversible results.

- Mary Shelley's *Frankenstein* is credited with being the first work of science fiction, followed by the novels of Jules Verne and H. G. Wells. H. G. Wells combined science with different strands of fantastic and speculative fiction to come up with romantic stories that lay outside of the known sphere of experience. Jules Verne used the technology of the day to suggest ways that science can provide directions for future thinking – eg., extraterrestrial travel and time travel.

- Niffenegger's approach to time travel is closer to the Wells perspective. She does not speculate about it but uses it to explore love and relationships. She has given us a story where two people are simply trying to live life together. Their problem is that one exists in the real world of time, while the other is unable to stay in time's real world. The fact that there is time travel in this novel does not necessarily make it science fiction. There are no magical or technological tricks to Henry's activities. But Niffenegger does leave us with a philosophical Wellsian perspective and asks, *What is time? How is it measured? Is time a tangible product that we can use, bend, spend?*

notes

- This novel lies on the boundary between science fiction and fantasy. Niffenegger wanted to write a story with some unbelievable elements, but she wanted to make them plausible. (A novel that uses a similar approach is Alice Sebold's *The Lovely Bones*.)

- Niffenegger finds Henry's time travel very plausible, and she works to fill the plot with as much reality as she can. In order to make this situation less bizarre, she looks at time travel as a genetic disorder. As her fascination grew, so did the story.

- Far from being science fiction, there are real and strange things that we know about or have all experienced, which seem to turn time on its head. Time is a man-made concept, and its measure is an arbitrary and pragmatic invention, which has changed radically over time.

## Style of Writing

- Niffenegger successfully combines scientific concepts and art to create a unique mechanism with which to tell her story. By using the idea of time travel, Niffenegger tells her story in a "disorderly" fashion. She looks at marriage in the way a cubist artist might see it – as seemingly unconnected parts that are unique to themselves but that fit together in an unconventional way. By taking the two perspectives of Henry and Clare and then breaking up the story chronologically, Niffenegger is able to create a "cubist" portrait of their relationship. She has created a wonderfully romantic book with an exceptional and distinct framework.

## Structure

- The novel has two distinct timelines for which Niffenegger kept two spreadsheets, one for each, in order to keep straight who is doing what, what each knows and doesn't know, and so forth. To keep things straight for herself, Niffenegger treated each scene as a separate puzzle piece that needed to move around before finding a place to fit. By breaking the story into individual scenes and perspectives, she allows the reader to consider the story according to its parts. Once the puzzle is complete, the whole picture is clear.

- In this sense, **The Time Traveler's Wife** can almost be considered two separate books, each mirroring the other as if they are coming from either side of the looking glass of time. The scenes are the same, but the individual perspective shifts the details, so that the "time" of each is different. Perhaps that is what real "time" is – a concept that is never the same for any of us!

- There are two narrative voices and perspectives (Henry's and Clare's), but the story itself unfolds in circular time. Events appear, then reappear later with explanation.

- The book is organized in three sections, plus a prologue. Each chapter is a visual scene, not a literary chapter. In this way, Niffenegger allows the details to emerge slowly. Each is a painting the reader views only by looking around and around the massive canvas. We are guided around the story mostly by Henry, but his narrative is totally intertwined with Clare's.

  o Part one ends with the wedding described by both Henry and Clare, on **pages 254-269** – *"and so, we are married."* Clare's past has finally caught up with Henry's present.

  o Part two has many dark moments, which include Clare's six miscarriages.

notes

- o Part three, which begins on p.495, details the essence of Henry's life and Clare's future. On p.499, we are given a third description of Henry being shot by hunters.

- The setting of the book is completely immersed in the Chicago that Niffenegger loves, so there are many wonderful details that evoke the music and the environment of the era.

# SYMBOLS

Dreams, Memories

Butterfly

Wings

Disappearance, Nakedness

Running

Cage, Death

Time Travel, (symbol)

# SYMBOLS

Niffenegger uses symbols that are immediately recognizable as symbols of love, freedom, and imagination. They are fragile (butterfly, wings), and intangible (dreams or memories), and they make sense. These symbols act as metaphors for the "disappearance" of the mind, not just the body. When Henry becomes *"stressed out, [he loses his] grip on now"* (p.306), his feelings are familiar to every reader. This is the power of Niffenegger's writing.

## Dreams, Memories

- Henry's first time travel experience was to the Field Museum of Natural History when he was five years old. His physical experience was one of being disconnected and floating. This feeling is much like ones we experience when we dream. As a matter of fact when he told his mother about this, she laughed and said that this time travel sounded like a wonderful, fun dream, and that she would like to try it too. But dreams are like fuzzy memories, so for the realists in the reading crowd, it is believable that Henry's experiences might have been a dream or the memory of a dream.

- Time travel gives Henry a *"feeling of unity, oblivion, mindlessness in the best sense of the word."* (p.25) When he is older, Henry drinks to excess in an effort to relive this lovely feeling. Another familiar situation. When he finds Clare, this feeling becomes connected to their relationship and Henry stops drinking.

- However, the fact that Clare is involved in Henry's memories makes this premise a bit troublesome. Clare has Henry beat up the guy who hits on her (p.92). **Is this her dream, her wish fulfillment?**

- There are a number of descriptions of Clare sleeping. Sleep erases time, and dreams mark time. *"Sleep is now my lover."* (p.501) It is only now through her dreams and memories that she can bring Henry back to life.

## Butterfly

- On Henry's visit to the Natural History Museum, he sees a beautiful blue butterfly called the Papili Ulysses, which travels and migrates across many time zones. Aside from the time travel, this butterfly reminds us of Homer's story of Ulysses and we are then thrust into many images – Henry traveling like Ulysses, Clare waiting patiently

like Penelope, Henry continually returning just like the butterfly to his place in time.

- The butterfly's wings are also part of the next symbol.

# Wings

- When Henry loses his feet to hypothermia (p.455), he loses his Achilles heel. Like the mythical Achilles, Henry needs his feet in order to run, to survive. Wings are the answer because wings will help move Henry to yet another stage or dimension. He is no longer able to move through time because he has used it all up. He also feels he has been *"abandoned by his protective angel."* (p.431)  Henry's angel in life was himself.

- All that Clare can do is to give him protective wings with which to transcend his immediate present and to enter his future.

> *The wings are huge and they float in the air, wavering in the candlelight. They are darker than the darkness, threatening but also redolent of longing, of freedom, of rushing through space. The feeling of standing solidly, on my own two feet, running like flying.* (p.466)

# Disappearance, Nakedness

- The incidence of Henry's disappearances can be connected to vanishing memories or dreams that disappear upon wakening. Niffenegger includes a number of things that disappear.

    o   Miscarried children. *"Where are they, these lost children, wandering, hovering around confused?"* **(p.334)** Niffenegger is questioning what happens to this lost energy. **Is it lost in time and space?**

    o   The present can disappear for example, when Gomez first sees Henry, he recognizes him and Henry feels *"a little bit of future seeping in."* **(p.422)**

    o   After his death, Henry will be held in the here and now only through Clare's and Alba's memories. Without this human ability to remember, life is simply a cycle of transformation. We travel out of our own life's seasons into our future. The change in this time transformation comes from within us. *"Time let me vanish."* **(p.515)**

- When Henry travels through time he always lands naked. Because he loses his clothes, he loses his connection to the time before. This is exactly the birth and death process. We begin and end in the same manner – the body is born naked, and the soul leaves unclothed by its body.

- Both Clare and Henry bleed – Clare from her many miscarriages, Henry from his wounds. In both instances, it is the blood of life that is draining away.

# Running

- Running is one of Niffenegger's best images, because we are all metaphorically trying to outrun time. Running as physical exertion has the effect of making you aware only of that moment in time. The physical act of running does both for Henry: it relieves his stress and anchors him in the here and now. Running gives Henry control over time. *"It is proof of my corporeal existence, my ability to control my movement through space, if not time..."* **(p.151)**

- In Henry's case, running becomes his religion. He runs as if his life depends on it.

# Cage, Death

- Niffenegger represents death through the image of the cage in Henry's library. We are told right from the beginning that if Henry ever finds himself in the cage, that will be his end. Indeed, there is no exit from the cage of death. But interestingly, the cage in the library is not completely enclosed – one can see into and out of its walls. Henry's co-workers are very curious about Henry and his odd behavior, but Henry dismisses their questions with the comment that no one would believe him if he told the truth. This raises another question about whether we believe only what we see. **Do we ignore what we don't believe and pretend that it does not exist?**

- Using the cage imagery, Niffenegger demonstrates the idea that perhaps the dead can see and be seen and that life and death continue along as an interactive relationship. However, in our own actual experiences, this is done through memories and through rememberences.

- When Henry is in the cage, he remembers or imagines the worst day in 1984, the day he is shot. Although he is actually shot in the past, it is the present world in which he dies. (p.429) His mind and his body finally come together in the same place, at the same time. We are meant to ask which death comes first, Henry's "virtual" death in the meadow or his real death on his forty-third birthday. *"I will know: somewhere out there I am dying."* (p.451, 452) (see Quantum theory, p.64)

- At the initial moment of his death process, Henry crashes into the living room in the midst of his party. Life and times are now a mess. Henry again suffers from hypothermia, which was responsible for his feet amputations. This also opens many questions about the mind's ability to endure greater pain and suffering than the body.

# Time Travel (symbol)

- Time can take many forms, and literature keeps up to date with all perspectives. In this century and in the last part of the twentieth century, literature has moved from portraying time as linear, to portraying it as a vertical or circular phenomenon. This is done through multiple narrations or through narratives that flow back and forth.

- Literature symbolizes time in a variety of ways. In this novel, we find memory, dreams, and the mind's confusion. Foreshadowing a future event is another literary technique that helps the reader see through present time into the future.

    *There are defining moments in our lives towards which time has run, but we don't know it. The moment is the goal.* (p.272)

- Time travel is what life is all about. While we are in the midst of the moment, we might possibly be aware of it, but in reality, we pass through it very quickly because we are busy. Once the moment is past, we relive it through memory. Time travel is a metaphorical link to the past, more so than to the future.

- Time is like a gas that can't be seen or felt, but we know it's there. It has no shape and we can't start or stop it. As we get closer to the end of it, time seems to race ahead, and at the end of the life process, the moment of death and time collide. This happens to Henry in the Monroe St. parking garage.

- Niffenegger uses time as an hourglass. Everyone is given a glass full of time, but its contents run out more quickly or more slowly for each person. Perhaps, like Henry, everyone knows when time begins to run out. *"I have a feeling, very familiar to me when I am out of time."* (p.502)

- Henry gives Clare the gift of future time when he tells her, *"We will see each other again ... until then live, fully present in the world which is so beautiful."* (p.504) His gift to her is the promise of hope and a life well lived. This was the reason for his list of dates, which also represented his promises to see her again. Henry also gives Alba a list of dates for when they will travel together. Because Alba is a new and future generation, she and Henry will be able to travel through time together.

notes

# LAST THOUGHTS

## Conclusion

## Time Travel (science)

## Quantum theory

# LAST THOUGHTS

## Conclusion

- Audrey Niffenegger has an extremely rich mix of interests and influences, many of which seem to come together in this highly original novel. It has been described as a "genre-bender" – a love story with a science fiction premise. Although she claims not to have a special interest in science fiction as such, she incorporates the science fiction idea of involuntary time travel into her story. She uses our built-in vulnerability and unease about the unknown of time travel to parallel the vulnerability to which we are exposed when we love.

- The novel has an alternative and edgy feel to it that also matches the mystery surrounding time travel. There are shades of herself as a punk youth that evoke the memories of the times in which she grew up. (see Punk, p.17) Although she did not go out much to the clubs that Henry and Ingrid frequented, she did listen to the music and paint her nails black. She has successfully included aspects of this alternative subculture and its worldview of attitude and independence in the character of Henry. Of all her characters, she relates most closely to Henry.

- **The Time Traveler's Wife** is more of a love story than anything else, but there are real elements of science fiction that are infused into the story. This reflects Niffenegger's intense curiosity into all things strange and mysterious.

# Time Travel    *the scientific idea*

We have talked about time travel as a literary concept and as a psychological/physical concept. (see Time, p.56 ) It also needs recognition as a scientific concept.

- In July 1976, the American Scout D rocket went into space with a special clock on board, an atomic clock whose purpose was to test whether time runs faster in space than it does on earth. The answer is yes and is based on Einstein's theory of relativity which depends on two concepts: speed and gravity.

- At the center of Einstein's theory is the nature of light and the fact that it travels ten thousand times faster than the most powerful rocket. This means that if a rocket were to be able to gather up enough speed, then the unexpected would be possible. When viewed from earth, we would see the expected – one rocket gaining on the other. Viewed from outer space, we would see the gap between them remain constant – the chase would last forever.

notes

o Another way to explain this to to consider that the idea of time is influenced, changed, and warped by light and by gravity. This gives us an extra dimension of perspective, known as the fourth dimension. In this dimension, light distorts the relationship between two objects and one of them is projected out of its normal sphere. One rocketship is real, the other is not.

o Because real time is so much slower than the speed of light, therefore, here on earth, the relativity factor is not so noticeable. But time can be warped by motion. The faster the speed, the greater the effect. (This is one reason Henry does not like airplanes.) The positive side is that because of the greater speed, travel in space takes less time therefore, there is less aging. We should all move to Mars!

o An absence of gravity also warps time. We know that clocks work differently in space, and in fact, a black hole is the stoppage of time. When a star implodes under its own gravity, it freezes everything in its vicinity. The light around it is also frozen and cannot move away from the object anymore. This is why the object appears to be black. To fall into a black hole is to travel beyond the end of time.

• The fact that time can stretch or shrink without limit opens up all sorts of philosophical and literary possibilities. If time has a beginning, then it must also have an end. Some astronomers believe that the entire universe will implode one day and fall out of time. When Henry dies, he falls into his own black hole and literally falls out of time.

• This is as simple as this guide can make it, but Niffenegger makes it even simpler. She asks that we suspend our disbelief and just accept what our hearts tell us.

notes

## Quantum Theory

- Quantum physics deals with science's view of the energy of matter by attempting to explain physical phenomena that cannot be explained through the classical theories of physics, which deal with the verifiable facts of gravity, orbit, wave particles of light, and especially the existence of the black hole.

- Quantum theory tries to prove that the nature of the universe is drastically different from what we think of it, how we feel, and what we think that we see. Niels Bohr, one of the scientists who developed the atom bomb, describes it in this way: *"Anyone who is not shocked by quantum theory has not understood it."*

- Niffenegger is not delving into this area as an explanation for time travel, but the theory of quantum physics hovers on the borders of her story and her characters. Her primary focus is to raise the possibility and plausibility of such a phenomenon. It makes a great story!

- There is a 2004 documentary film that functions as an excellent, but basic, guide to quantum theory, which may be of interest to Niffenegger's readers. It is titled *What the Bleep Do We Know!* and stars Marlee Matlin.

# FROM THE NOVEL

# FROM THE NOVEL ...

## Memorable Quotes from the Text of

## *The Time Traveler's Wife*

**PAGE 8.** I am speechless. Here is Henry, calm, clothed, younger than I have ever seen him. Henry is working at the Newberry Library, standing in front of me, in the present ...

... I'm flooded with years of knowledge of Henry, while he's looking at me perplexed and fearful. [Clare]

**PAGE 17.** 'I had no idea you were a librarian. You made it impossible for me to find you in the present; you said it would just happen when it was supposed to happen, and here we are.' [Clare]

**PAGE 24.** Outside it's chilly. Cars and cyclists cruise along Dearborn while couples stroll down the sidewalks and there we are with them, in the morning sunlight, hand in hand, finally together for anyone to see. I feel a tiny pang of regret, as though I've lost a secret, and then a rush of exaltation: now everything begins. [Clare]

**PAGE 31, 32.** 'It's okay, Henry. I'm your guide, I'm here to show you around. It's a special tour. Don't be afraid, Henry.'

notes

'This is a special tour, only for you, because it's your birthday. Besides, grown-ups don't do this sort of thing.'

'Aren't you a grown up?'

'I'm an extremely unusual grown-up. My job is to have adventures. So naturally when I heard that you wanted to come back to the Field Museum right away, I jumped at the chance to show you around.' [Henry]

**PAGE 38.**   I hesitate. Clare is content, absorbed. She must be about six ... I wonder if today is the day we are supposed to meet for the first time or if it's some other day. Maybe I should be very silent and either Clare will go away and I can go munch up those apples and steal some laundry or I will revert to my regularly scheduled programming. [Henry}

**PAGE 50.**   I am standing across the street from the Art Institute of Chicago on a sunny June day in 1973 in the company of my nine-year-old self. He is traveling from next Wednesday; I have come from 1990. We have a long afternoon and evening to frivol as we will, and so we have come to one of the great art museums of the world for a little lesson in pickpocketing.

'Can't we just look at the art?' pleads Henry. He's nervous. He's never done this before.

'Nope. You need to know this. How are you going to survive if you can't steal anything?' [Henry]

**PAGE 63.**   We are both touching the thing very lightly, we are trying to do it right and not push. Then it starts to move, slow. It goes in circles, and then stops on H.   Then it speeds up. E, N, R, Y. 'Henry,' says Mary Christine, 'who's Henry?" ... Just as I'm thinking I'm safe, the plastic thing starts to move. H, it says ... Then it goes on: U, S, B, A, N, D.   [Clare]

**PAGE 72.**   Henry says he comes from the future. When I was little I didn't see any problem with that ... Now I wonder if it means that the future is a place, or like a place, that I could go to; that is go to in some way other than just getting older.   [Clare]

**PAGE 76, 77.** 'I'm constantly running up against the fact that I can't change anything, even though I am right there, watching it.'

'But Henry, you do change things! I mean, you wrote down that stuff that I'm supposed to give you in 1991 about the baby with Down Syndrome. And the List, if I didn't have the List I would never know when to come meet you. You change things all the time.' ...

[Clare] rolls her eyes. 'What is the opposite of determinism?'

'Chaos ... Chaos is more freedom; in fact, total freedom. But no meaning. I want to be free to act, and I also want my actions to mean something.' [Henry]

**PAGE. 110.** Clare is all ears; she's always eager for any bits of autobiography I let drop. As the dates on the List grow few and our two years of separation loom large, Clare is secretly convinced she can find me in real time if I would only dole out a few facts. Of course, she can't, because I won't, and she doesn't. [Henry]

**PAGE 117.** I have a sudden glimpse of all the Christmases of my life lined up one after another, waiting to be gotten through, and despair floods me ... I wish for a moment that Time would lift me out of this day, and into some more benign one. But then I feel guilty for wanting to avoid the sadness; dead people need us to remember them ... even if all we can do is say I'm sorry until it is as meaningless as air. [Henry]

**PAGE 147.** As I wrap my hair in a towel I see myself blurred in the mirror by steam and time seems to fold over onto itself and I see myself as a layering of all my previous days and years and all the time that is coming and suddenly I feel as though I've become invisible. But then the feeling is gone as fast as it came and I stand still for a minute and then I pull on my bathrobe and open the door and go on. [Clare]

**PAGE 212.** As I stand in the foyer fumbling for my key Mrs. Kim peeps out of her door and furtively gestures for me to step in. I am alarmed; Kimy is usually very hearty and loud and affectionate, and although she knows everything there is to know about us she never interferes. Well, almost never. Actually, she gets pretty involved in our lives, but we like it. I sense that she is really upset. [Henry]

**PAGE 239.** Henry looks at me ... Then he says, quite seriously, 'On an EEG, I have the brain of a schizophrenic. More than one doctor has insisted that this little time-travel delusion of mine is due to schizophrenia.' [Clare]

**PAGE 249.** Henry says, 'Whatever happens, we both know that I live to be at least forty-three. So don't worry about it.'

Forty-three? 'What happens after forty-three?'

'I don't know, Clare. Maybe I figure out how to stay in the present.' He gathers me in and we are quiet. [Clare]

**PAGE 255.** I wake up in my bed, the bed of my childhood. As I float on the surface of waking I can't find myself in time ... I have been dreaming all night. The dreams merge, now. In one part of this dream I was swimming in the ocean, I was a mermaid ...[on a sailboat was my mother] I swam up to her and she was surprised to see me there, she said <u>Why Clare, I thought you were getting married today,</u> and I suddenly realized, the way you do in dreams, that I couldn't get married to Henry if I was a mermaid, and I started to cry, and then I woke up and it was the middle of the night. [Clare]

**PAGE 313.** When Henry and I had been married for about two years we decided, without talking about it very much, to see if we could have a baby. I knew that Henry was not at all optimistic about our chances ... and I was not asking him or myself why this might be because I was afraid that he had seen us in the future without any baby and I just didn't want to know about that. [Clare]

**PAGE 339.** I'm so tired. I'm tired of thinking about death. I'm tired of sex as a means to an end. And I'm frightened of where it all might end. I don't know how much pressure I can take from Clare.

What are these fetuses, these embryos, these clusters of cells we keep making and losing? ... Nature is telling us to give up, Nature is saying: Henry, you're a very fucked-up organism and we don't want to make any more of you. [Henry]

**PAGE 388.** ... I push and Alba's head comes out and I put my hand down to touch her head, her delicate slippery wet velvet head and I push and push and Alba tumbles into Henry's waiting hands ... I am empty and released ... and then Alba yells out and suddenly she is here, someone places her on my belly, and I look down ... [Clare]

**PAGE 395.** This is a secret: sometimes I am glad when Henry is gone. Sometimes I enjoy being alone. Sometimes I walk through the house late at night and I shiver with the pleasure of not talking, not touching, just walking, or sitting, or taking a bath ...

Sometimes I am glad when Henry's gone, but I'm always glad when he comes back. [Clare]

**PAGE 421.** Ingrid and I are at the Riviera Theater, dancing our tiny brains out to the dulcet tones of Iggy Pop. Ingrid and I are always happiest together when we are dancing or fucking or anything else that involves physical activity and no talking. Right now we are in heaven ... the concert finally ends ... I'm watching a yuppie in a BMW argue with a valet-parking kid over an illegal space when this huge blond guy walks up to me. [Henry]

**PAGE 429, 430.** It was early. A day in the fall. Daddy and Mark were out deer hunting. I woke up; I thought I heard you calling me, and I ran out into the meadow and you were there, and you and Daddy and Mark were all looking at something, but Daddy made me go back to the house, so I never saw what you were looking at. [Clare]

**PAGE 436.** It's my forty-third birthday. My eyes pop open at 6:46 a.m. even though I have the day off from work, and I can't get back to sleep ... Ordinarily, I am expert at shaving without actually looking at myself, but today, in honor of my birthday, I take inventory.

notes

My hair has gone almost white ... My skin is wind-roughened and there are creases at the edges of my eyes ... My face is too thin. All of me is too thin ... Early stages of cancer thin, perhaps. Heroin addict, thin. I don't want to think about it, so I continue shaving. [Henry]

**PAGE 440.** I come to in the dark, on a cold concrete floor. I try to sit up, but I get dizzy and I lie down again. My head is aching. I explore with my hands; there's a big swollen area just behind my left ear. As my eyes adjust, I see the faint outlines of stairs, and Exit signs, and far above me a lone fluorescent bulb emitting cold light. All around me is the criss-crossed steel pattern of the Cage. I'm at the Newberry, after hours, inside the Cage. [Henry]

**PAGE 445, 446.** I explain about causal loops, and quantum mechanics and photons and the speed of light. I explain about how it feels to be living outside of the time constraints most humans are subject to. I explain about the lying, and the stealing, and the fear. I explain about trying to have a normal life ...

'Without Clare I would have given up a long time ago,' I say. 'I never understood why Clark Kent was so hell bent on keeping Lois Lane in the dark'

'It makes a better story,' says Matt.

'Does it? I don't know,' I reply. [Henry]

**PAGE 454.** 'Help me!' I yell. No one comes. I curl into a ball in front of the door, bring my knees to my chin, wrap my hands around my feet. No one comes, and then, at last, at last, I am gone. [Henry]

**PAGE 469.** In my dream I am running. Everything is fine. I run along the lake ... But things begin to go wrong. Parts of my body are falling off ... I roll and roll until I roll into the lake, and the waves roll me under, and I wake up gasping. [Henry]

**PAGE 486.** ... tonight my life will flash before my eyes. We've invited everyone who matters to us ... the only people missing have been unavoidably detained: my mother, Lucille, Ingrid ... Oh, God. Help me. [Henry]

**PAGE 500.** The living room is very still. Everyone stands fixed, frozen, staring down at us ... I sit on the floor, holding Henry ... Henry's skin is warm, his eyes are open, staring past me, he is heavy in my arms, so heavy, his pale skin torn apart, red everywhere, ripped flesh framing a secret world of blood. I cradle Henry. There's blood at the corner of his mouth. I wipe it off. [Clare]

**PAGE. 501.** Sometime I wake up and reach for Henry. Sleep erases all differences: then and now; dead and living. [Clare]

**PAGE 502-504.** Dearest Clare,

As I write this, I am sitting at my desk in the back bedroom looking out at your studio ... I have the feeling, ... of being buoyed up by time ... I suddenly wanted to leave something, for <u>after</u> ... I hate to think of you waiting. I know that you have been waiting for me all of your life ... We will see each other again, Clare. Until then, live, fully, present in the world, which is so beautiful.

It's dark, now, and I am very tired. I love you, always. Time is nothing.

Henry

# ACKNOWLEDGEMENTS

# ACKNOWLEDGEMENTS

Altomare, Scott (and others), producer. William Arntz (and others), director. *What The Bleep Do We Know?* a film shot in the U.S.A., 2004. [Also known as *What the #$*! Do We Know!?*]

Crelinsten, Jeffrey, *'The Race to Test Relativity'.* Ideas, The Toronto Star. Toronto, October 9, 2005.

Epstein, Daniel Robert. *'Audrey Niffenegger – The Time-Traveler's Wife'.* Interview for suicidegirls.com

Flanagan, Mark. *'Audrey Niffenegger Interview'* – December 7, 2003. www.contemporarylit.about.com

Hillegas, Mark R. *'H.G. Wells'.* Twentieth-Century Literary Criticism, Vol. 19. Gale Research, Inc. Detroit, 1967.

MacDonald, Gayle, *'I have a natural Goth Sensibility.'* Globe Review, The Globe and Mail. Toronto, November 22, 2005.

Merriam Webster's Reader's Handbook, Merriam-Webster, Inc., Springfield, Massachusetts, 1997.

The New Illustrated Science and Invention Encyclopedia, *'Exploring the fourth dimension'.* H.S. Stuttman Inc. Publishers, Vol. 21. Westport Connecticut, 1989.

Rabkin, Eric S., *Science Fiction.* Nineteenth-Century Literature Criticism, Vol.24. Gale Research, Inc. Detroit, 1989.

Thurlbeck, Gregg, **Rambles, Cultural Arts Magazine.** *'The Time Traveler's Wife'.* www.rambles.net   Nov. 20, 2004.

Zambreno, Kate. *'Audrey Niffenegger: Woman on the edge of time'* Newcity Magazine, Chicago, January 2004.